BACKYARD ANIMALS
SNAKES

by Genevieve Nilsen

TABLE OF CONTENTS

Words to Know 2

Snakes 3

Let's Review! 16

Index 16

WORDS TO KNOW

blue

gray

green

orange

red

yellow

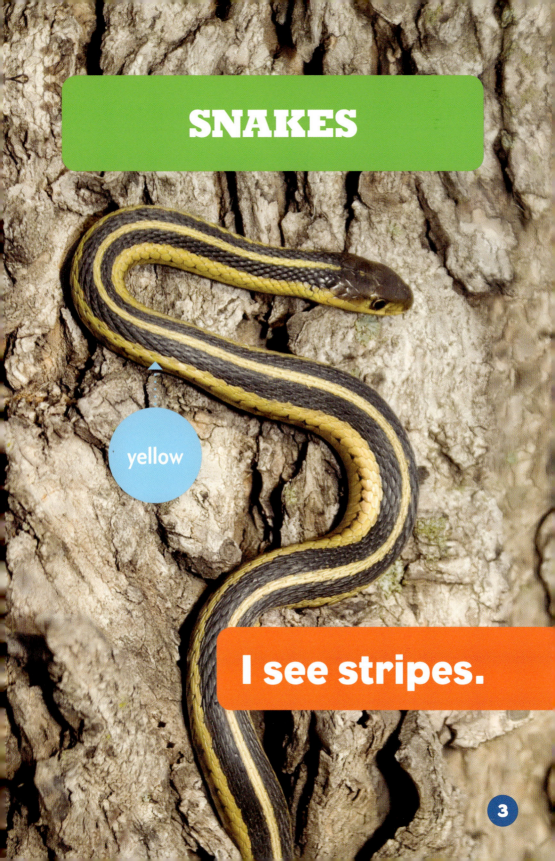

SNAKES

yellow

I see stripes.

I see stripes.

blue

I see stripes.

orange

I see stripes.

I see stripes.

gray

I see stripes.

white

I see stripes.

LET'S REVIEW!

Not all backyard snakes have stripes. What color is this snake?

INDEX

blue 6
gray 12
green 4
orange 8

red 10
stripes 3, 5, 7, 9, 11, 13, 15
white 14
yellow 3